Like Magic but Real

Maryam Daftari

Like Magic but Real
Maryam Daftari

Copyright © 2015 Maryam Daftari

Published by 1st World Publishing
P.O. Box 2211, Fairfield, Iowa 52556
tel: 641-209-5000 • fax: 866-440-5234
web: www.1stworldpublishing.com

First Edition
LCCN: 2015902169
ISBN: 978-1-4218-3722-2

This material has been written and published for educational purposes to enhance one's well-being. In regard to health issues, the information is not intended as a substitute for appropriate care and advice from health professionals, nor does it equate to the assumption of medical or any other form of liability on the part of the publisher or author. The publisher and author shall have neither liability nor responsibility to any person or entity with respect to loss, damages, or injury claimed to be caused directly or indirectly by any information in this book.

To my beloved Mother and Father

Contents

Nature's Play

Windows

Acknowledgements

I would like to express my thanks to all who made this book possible. My deep gratitude goes first and foremost to my son, Ali Arsanjani, who has always been my source of encouragement and support. Without his help, comments, and feedback this book would never have seen the light of day.

I am indebted to many of my fellow poets and members of the Society of Great River Poets of Iowa, especially Rodney Reeves, Ron Kahl, and Mary Zachmeyer who have not only inspired me, but have taken the time to review and give feedback on this manuscript. Rod's unique leadership and organizing abilities have kept the poetry society functioning and lively. Special thanks to him for his thought provoking comments and suggestions. Mary's perceptive commentaries were especially welcome. Thanks to all the members, who, over the years, have read and commented on my poems during our poetry sessions in Burlington and Mount Pleasant, Iowa. Many of these poems have been published in the Society's two publications: *A Step Between* and *Stand Forth*.

I wish to especially thank Lucille Morgan Wilson, Iowa's gifted poet and tireless editor of *Lyrical Iowa* for carefully reading and commenting on my manuscript.

Fairfield poet Bill Graeser, notorious for reciting his poems from memory, has also provided valuable feedback.

I would also like to thank poet and author, Steve Kowit, my mentor and friend in San Diego who through his invaluable workshops and our e-mail exchanges continues to guide me on my poetic journey.

Special thanks are due to Rodney Charles, dear friend and publisher in Fairfield, Iowa.

Foreword

Take a journey

a journey of compassion

a journey of challenge

Maryam Daftari takes us on this journey through her collection of poems, *Like Magic But Real.* On this journey you'll find the mystic and spiritual side of existence, explore the caves you may never have gone into and hear stories from our collective past

In *Hold Back the Creeping Darkness*, Daftari implores us to "catch it before it silences the light", giving us permission, indeed command, to resist powers of darkness. She explores the Sufi mystic relationship of the moth and flame in *The Candle and the Moth's Love Affair*, reflecting on the all too human attraction to someone (or something) which may not be good for you,

Throughout this volume you will receive encouragement and challenge to "be like ordinary stone," "with the people," to "see the rose" in yourself and others.

You will be encouraged to imagine "how the soul feels" while your human self is going through good and difficult situations. Daftari explores many aspects of nature, from *The Butterfly* to *The Bamboo*, *Garden Spider* to the moon, and particularly their effect on humans and vice-versa.

With humor and sensitivity, Daftari combines these attributes like few poets are able to, with a nod to nature:

Nature always seems to have its act together
never missing a single performance or cue
as we are apt to do;

Rod Reeves,
Society of Great River Poets, Iowa

Introduction

Like Magic but Real is a quest, at times mystical, in search of understanding life's mysteries and Nature's miracles as they unfold within our daily lives. Poetry speaks from one heart to another, from my heart to your heart. There are times when the soul takes over from the heart and mind, leading us along the mystical dimensions of life.

In this collection of poems, I share my feelings and emotional bond with Nature by trying to capture a tiny fraction of its infinite beauty and variety. My eyes and ears, mind and heart, join in the symphony of displaying the magical but real panorama surrounding us: the baffling questions we are all challenged with and sometimes find difficult to process. Some poems recount the spectacular performance of Nature's varied designs and plays, and how life has blessed us with unexpected miracles, despite the challenges, ups and downs and diverse experiences we have encountered.

We are influenced by our culture, traditions, and environment in varying degrees. From childhood and throughout my adult life, in addition to the great English and American poets I studied, I was also surrounded by the mystical poetry of great Persian poets, such as Rumi, Hafez, and Omar Khayyam – through my parents, teachers, and friends. I heard them quote the esthetically appealing rhythmic flow of their poems which motivated me to study them myself. The beauty and powerful eloquence of their verses brought me immeasurable pleasure, inspiring me to appreciate and ultimately write poetry.

I owe so much to my parents who taught me, by example, to enjoy literature, especially poetry. They encouraged me from an early age to try my hand at creative writing. During my undergraduate and graduate years, although I became fascinated with Chinese affairs, majoring in political science and international relations – ultimately leading me to become a Sinologist – my heart and joy remained in poetry. Chinese philosophy and culture have also influenced my way of thinking and have sometimes found an outlet in my poetry. As a student of Chinese affairs, I published three books and over 25 articles on China. Even though I enjoyed writing poetry as an undergraduate and won several awards, I restarted writing poetry in earnest after the passing of my parents in 1985 and 1994.

One of the goals in publishing this book is to share

with you, the fulfilling joy I have felt in creating each poem and how I humbly hope you will ponder with me on the sometimes intangible phenomena of life. We can search for answers, in a way, together by accessing more inspiration and light in our lives. Poems are successful if and when they have the power to make us smile or laugh, or help us dive deep within, to inspire and challenge us to think about the mysteries – apparent or hidden – encircling us.

Poems are our faithful companions throughout life. Attracting us with their literary magnetism, they can speak to us like true friends. We take refuge in them in times of sorrow. We rejoice with them in times of joy. They can communicate specific meaning and music to us. And so I write to share with you my innermost thoughts. Each poem may have a message to challenge our way of thinking. Each poem asks whether we have alternative ways of looking at universal questions. This is especially true for the first (*Quest*) and second (*Nature's Play*) sections.

The third and last section (*Windows*), although sprinkled with personal life experiences, is there not only to share them with you, but to perhaps inspire you to ponder and relate them to your own unique experiences, sometimes painful, sometimes inspiring – intimate cathartic feelings like I am sharing with you. This can be a healing process – an honest painting of a life lived the best way we can at the time – whether colorful or dark. Each experience is different and instructive. Poems are ultimately there to share and evoke emotions, stimulating us to think either in a similar vein or to take another side of an issue. We may not remember the exactly words of a poem but we can often recall its meaningful message. And sometimes the heart has already memorized it. We are all seekers in search of answers, and like devoted detectives, we like to decipher the hidden messages in poems.

It is in the nature of the human spirit to dive into the transcendent, to meditate on both the simple and the complex. We all have dreams, sometimes close to the realm of reality, or sometimes the magical – that makes us soar above our daily routines – where we sometimes yearn for them to become real in some way. Poems can open doors to what we as seekers of truth search for. Life is full of mysteries and we are sometimes confronted with or given alternative ways of seeing past the veil.

We often write because we hope that a poem will affect the reader in some positive way. If it affects a person profoundly, then it is a blessing! If a poem can win the reader's attention and open a window toward a truth or show how it is possible to view something in an entirely different light, the writer will have achieved her or his purpose. Maybe a poem can unlock something in our innermost being causing an *aha* moment of exhilaration. This can be powerful and transformative. Many of us may have had the experience of reveling in secret bliss – when we recite verses from our favorite poets. We draw inspiration or comfort from a poet's vision, and some poems may challenge our long-held assumptions. If my poems have accomplished even one of the above, I would consider myself fulfilled.

Maryam Daftari

Carlsbad, CA
January 1, 2015

Quest

And so we wander on a journey of possible discoveries paved with many questions. We may traverse along mystical territory, sometimes not apparent to the senses or to our reasoning intellect. That is why I call this first section, Quest: inquiries into domains of the transcendent, the Divine, the silent witness – the soul, the knowing heart and the restless mind, and our search for Love and Light. We ponder on the Creator's Design, fate, truth, happiness and bliss – the eternal twins. All such queries seek answers. Some of the poems reveal not only the influence of Persian mystical poets, especially of Rumi on my poetry, but also of how Chinese philosophy has impacted my way of thinking. These poems all contain spiritual issues I have grappled with and tried to fathom in my own way.

In My House of Love

In my house of love,
I am inside a golden cocoon of bliss

You can join me here
if you find

the
  golden entrance
          thread.

The Present

The present is
   an enduring gift
      don't duel with it—
         the sword is useless.

I Shed Tears like a Candle

I
shed
hot tears
like a burning
candle,
For
I
know
my days are numbered,
The moth circles
the burning candle,
Warmed by the
love of the light and
the tears of the beloved flame;
So I patiently circle
life day and night
in my yearning heart and soul,

for a glimmer of the
Light of the Beloved.

Am I Alone?

Before arising,
I ask myself:
"Am I alone?"

And the answer flashes:
"Not when your mind
first thinks of God

and your heart
opens to the Divine."

Secrets

If you are in my heart,
   I can trust you,

But there are still things
   I cannot tell you;

I am glad that a veil
   Hides my secrets from you,

For I only want God
   To see behind the veil.

The Mind Needs Scrubbing

The mind needs scrubbing
  It is restless, undecided and tarnished
The soul is the pure trustworthy pearl
  Unrivalled, unbiased spark of the Divine

And where is the heart in all this?
  It runs from one to the other
Trying to keep the peace
  It cares about our wandering

Unbridled thoughts
  It comforts the lone soul
And searches for a balance
  Between mind and soul

Yet only the soul has the magic
  Wand of virtue and purity
It tries to scrub the mind clean
  To sweep its darkness away

To polish it like a mirror
  So the heart can see
The reflection and smile
  With the knowing soul.

I Will Dig Up the Mountain

I will dig up the mountain just to find my Self
Ignoring the bleeding sarcasm of razor-sharp tongues

I will sometimes swallow rain drops, sometimes the sun
Then I shall weep the rain or burn my heart to ashes

I will pour the ocean's water into my thirsty soul
And pray for redemption from the doubting clergy

I will douse my passion and curb my pride
Dreaming of a consciousness bathed in bliss

And in all this turmoil – the soul
Stands steadfast – it is soaked in love

Always there for my Self – wiser than the wisest.

The Candle and Moth's Love Affair*

Don't behead the candle
let it cry its sorrows of love away

saying farewell to the faithful moth
who sacrifices its life

in search of Love and Light –
does the candle's blazing flame

lure the passionate moth
or does the moth ultimately

seduce the fiery candle –
together to complete

the dance of love?

*In some Eastern cultures, and especially in Sufi mystical
poetry, it is common to write about the image of the moth
adoringly flying around the burning candle. It symbolizes our
love and search for the Divine.

Do You Dream Your Life?

Do you dream your life
　in a cup
　　of crimson wine

or do you ask
　the dark tea leaves
　　its planted secrets?

does your heart
　show you the compass
　　of your life?

does the bee
　bubble honey into
　　your bitter memories?

does the shadow
　foretell an approaching
　　darkness of fate?

or the sunshine
  dazzle – revealing
    the sweetness of eternity?

do the angels pick
  and cook your fate foods
    changing the ingredients

on your karma charts?

The Gift

When we get up in the morning
   the day is gifted to us on a clean slate –
a pregnant void, field of all possibilities

open to our unintelligible scribbles
   or yearning to be filled with elegant calligraphy

an unwrapped box waiting to be filled with surprises
   we can pack it with our dreams
or put someone's hopes into it, maybe our own

it's an empty stage on which we perform our dream plays
   where we are script writer, director, hero:

all are waiting for *us* to act
   regardless, the day and the Play unfold
yet without our fire, the stage is dark

perhaps someone will receive that gift
   and maybe we shall get a standing ovation!

The Silent Witness

I wonder what the soul feels
   when we laugh and snuggle in our bliss

I wonder how it feels
   when we freeze in our sorrows' numbness

When happy, the soul takes our hand
   like a proud partner and leads us
     in a dance of love,

It can shift gears, becoming the comforter
   when we grieve and pine,
     hugging us like a caring parent –

That ever sleepless silent witness.

Divine Design

He creates us worthy so we can carve our own lives
like a sculptor molding statues, playing with clay

Endowing us with all we need – gifting us
with varying doses of wisdom and ability

Blessing us with Divine grace so we can forge
if we want – masterpieces of our lives

Shaping each day lovingly like a sculptor at work
chiseling away at the challenges of creating

We shape it just the way we dream it
with patience, effort and skill

Beautiful like a work of Michelangelo or one likely
to be disposed of into the bin of oblivion

Or something in between where most of us seem
to be – depending on skillful crafting hands

And the ever present spark of grace from above
to create and cast what is worthy and noble

Distilled down to our God-given innate creativity –
the determining factor –

Inherited from the Master Sculptor's image.

Hold Back the Creeping Darkness

Hold back the creeping darkness
   catch it before it silences the light

Agitate not those at restful hiatus
   a dream is a lucent gift to guard

Let the saintly transform the godless
   turning the unholy to God's light

Behold the careless ruse of the unwise
   yet welcomed in the sage's embrace.

The Monk

The monk, sufi,
seer, dervish,
and the enlightened

rich in their poverty –
dwelling in God-consciousness
abode of the truly rich.

Who yearns for
the poverty of riches –
those that tempt?

Some souls search and reach
only for the riches of poverty –
those that dwindle not.

A monk with his spiritual wealth can feel
like a king – but a king cannot live
like a dervish or monk.

The Heart Needs No Sun

The heart needs
  no sun or moon
    to light its path

there is no darkness there –
  it is soaked in
    the light of love

and finds its path
  through sacrifice,
    ignoring love's frustrations

a true lover is never lost
  down this winding love path.

Yesterday, Today, Tomorrow

Today is your to-do day

Tomorrow is your dream day

Yesterday is forgotten – mostly

What ties them together

      is the long strong
           chain of hope.

Triumph of Souls

Can there ever be a dark spot in some souls?
Never – only in the murky mind

Are all souls alike in strength and purity?
Capable to withstand the mind's twists and turns?

Do some have their somber sides?
Prone sometimes to shades of grey?

Does the mischief of the mind
Wrestle with the heart and soul?

And do they shed tears of sorrow
When the erratic mind turns a blind eye?

Can we clear away the mind's clouds
And submit to the sunny soul we are born with

To hold back the creeping darkness?
The soul's spark of the Divine can kindle

The fading flame of the mind
And become the mind's savior –

Its rays illuminating –
Banishing the darkness.

Happiness or Bliss?

Happiness 'apparates'* from the outside
  jumps in and slams the door –
    capricious as a child,

bliss bubbles from inside the soul
  partnering with the loving heart
    tranquil and soaring in unison,

happiness and bliss, the eternal twins
  unwavering waves of the halcyon
    ocean-heart – serene yet cascading –

perpetuating joy of Self.

*Apparates is a term used by J .K. Rowling in her Harry Potter
books signifying the transport of a person from one location
to another.

Jade or Ordinary Stone

Which am I –
jade or ordinary stone?

The Taoist says:
"Don't be like jade,
be like ordinary stone."

I like shiny jade,
especially the green –
it's like a proud leader

but alone, unconnected,
waiting to be praised;

the stone is forever,
humble, simple
with many companions,

I would rather be
with the people.

Love Sees the Rose

Love only sees the rose
  and not the thorn.
Love waits and is patient

uncovering the good
  shutting its eyes to the bad.
Love may seem blind

yet it sees and seeks the truth
  searching to serve
like a faithful friend

a gem that grows more precious
  the longer you have it.
Love does not bargain –

it only accepts, surrendering in peace.
  Love redeems, transforming lives.
It heals like the Healer,

effortless, performing like a miracle worker.
 It's always there –
in our hearts and souls.

Brooding Moods

Every brooding thought of transitioning
to the other side descends on one's mood like a
black cloud that parachutes over our heads
and sometimes does not go away –
a sense of foreboding, a creeping
darkness clouds the heart like a
gathering storm foretelling imminent disaster.

After sailing through our forties and fifties
and climbing up to the mid-sixties and beyond
farewells become as common as hellos
left and right, friends and family start their
homeward journeys as horses galloping to stalls.
Are we used tea leaves ready to be dumped?
Does God send His angels to pick us like flowers?

We are never ready to go, like students
unprepared and dreading the final exams.
Do we stand brave and firm on Judgment Day
tranquil and confident of the Creator's grace or
more like a crying baby not knowing that
when we lose one breast of milk,
we are given the other to nourish us?

The hourglass is always set on automatic –
it fills fast, yet we are given new ones to fill,
we are granted another chance and yet another
like spoiled children loved and forgiven.
Still some fear the end, as if it were the razor's edge,
akin to confronting an enemy or an inescapable plague,
we hang on to dear life like a desperate cliffhanger.

Is life as we know it really racing to the finish line?
Is it just a self-induced dread of impending calamity,
a weakening of faith, or a fear of the unknown?

Truth is a Peddler

In ancient times
truth was absolute
but only for a few –
the prophets and seers of truth.

"Truth is mighty and will prevail!"*
Yet for many of us these days
truth seems more like a peddler
drifting from place to place

from mind to mind
sometimes unclaimed
a restless vagabond
an outlaw at times.

Truth is a peddler
uttering "take me in"
accepted or suppressed
rejected, bought and sold

an impartial judge you tend to ignore
neglect or shut off,
arrest it and you jail yourself
free it from the cage

and the heart snatches it
sometimes it's hidden
abandoned, stained, twisted
persecuted, kicked around

trampled on, dressed as falsehoods
just as lies are packaged, sold as 'truths'
it is illusive, yet reachable
sometimes homeless, always humble

priceless like enlightenment.
We yearn for it, search for it,
and yes, even die for it –
somctimes on a cross.

*In Latin, "*Magna est veritas et praevalet.*"

Light the Shadows

There is so much light within
    gone unnoticed
to both share and keep for eternity.

The mind's hurricane speeds on –
    the soul's addictive stillness stays.
Find the right key to crack open

the unexplained mysteries
    uncovering a passion to lead
far away from harm's way –

to weave the delicate tapestry
    of your life with no broken
seams of promises.

Write the book of your tomorrows
    and the days after
flowing like a winding stream

the way you dream them,
   with more light seeping in to see
love's waiting reflection

like an ever-burning candle.
   Let the trapped lightning inside
leap into your lap ready

to radiate this inner light outward
   like fireworks – to light
the shadowed paths

of unfulfilled karma.

Eternity

At the edge of eternity
you can burn all deadlines.
The eye witnesses sacred times and places
of your innermost dreams.

The seeming mazes of life
melt like spring ice
leaving time on your hands.
You hold heaven's unbroken maps,

mazed maps you could not read
in the walled city of your life.
Immortal treasures lost,
your faults get laundered

by the purity of celestial light.
Now you can dispose
of all your clothes and makeup,
for in eternity, pure beauty
of nakedness shines,
mirroring all like magic.

Crystal Ball

The liar's crystal ball
gradually reveals all

You don't have to wait
for signs of storm or malice
You suspected
unobtrusive treachery

"Mischief thou art afoot
Take thou what course thou wilt"

Coming through like
a mirror image in the water
wickedness splashing
like dark waves on the shore

Deception stands
naked and cold
drenched in the
emperor's new clothes.

I witness all.

Julius Caesar, Act 3, Scene 2, P 11.

Gasps

When my heart skips too many beats, too many times,
as if hooked on love

When my breath seems to stop in awe
like a candle blown out by the wind

When the star jasmine's delicate fragrance
descends on my senses – hypnotizing me

When the coral, emerald, agate, and topaz
sparkling in jewelry store windows

Reflect memories of the sun's glittering rays
on dancing fall leaves

My heart and soul takes them all in –
swallowing them slowly,

in dreamy gasps of gratitude.

I Curl Inside My Warm Cocoon

I curl again inside my warm cocoon
Away from the cruel blizzard outside
Sensing that I need to go there

And stay in this quiet blissful state
A kind of "dangling state" of now –
To be with myself, alone, satisfied.

A suspension in time and space
I want to dwell here indefinitely
Sensing a feeling of not wanting

Except remaining in this solitary mode
With an awareness of not needing anything –
A cozy feeling to keep this Iowa winter.

Nature's Play

Just like Nature's, our thoughts and minds may be characterized by intricate patterns and designs. Nature and our lives are inextricably bound together. We live in and with Nature, and we learn from Nature. We even have to design our lives so as to be in harmony with Nature. The seasons determine so much of what we can or cannot do. Nature brings us pleasure, sometimes sorrow. She bestows the blessings of beauty on our eyes, but may also rain catastrophe on our heads. This is what I hope to portray in Nature's Play.

Poems in this section glide us through the ever-enfolding wonders around us. Nature is – like magic but real! We will follow the butterfly, the weeping willow, the "Zen" duck, the squirrel, the garden spider, the bamboo, the hummingbird, the Iowa freezing rain, even the sun and the moon. We will watch the jousting of winter and spring and witness their painting contest. We shall revel in the beauty of the seasons, and embrace the lesson of Nature's flow. We are one with all!

The Butterfly

The butterfly adorns all,
alighting lightly on a
shocking pink flower
only to catch its breath
and take to flight again,
choosing now a daffodil
as its golden throne
to grace it with a quick flicker
of its black polka- dotted
yellow silk skirt.

Then in a fanciful sweep
hovering over purple pansies
giddy with a drunken daze,
the butterfly glides over a meadow
of blood crimson tulips,
flapping its fragile wings
for the final destined soft landing
and comfort of its eternal rest –

surrendering to Nature's cycle.

Micro-warrior

Still half asleep, I slowly open my bedroom shades
to find a hummingbird staring at me
as if stuck to the windowpane,

Was it trying to bring me the eternal message
of courage and hope from the universe or was it
admiring its own reflection in the windowpane?

This iridescent, green, five gram gem
fiercely independent, territorial and tough
has stolen my heart, mesmerizing me

into following it day after day, here and there.
I've witnessed this tiny fearless bird attacking
a hawk, chasing it out of its guarded terrain,

preferring to have its one-pointed focus
on dipping its syringe-like beak and long tongue
into flowers like a surgeon inserting a needle –
sucking sap, pollen, or nectar, alternating these
with prized protein-mouthfuls of insects.

It flies like a combination of a flying dart
and a spinning top – hovering now
sucking on the nectar of the pink zinnia,
a red hibiscus or the bell-shaped orange
flowers of an aloe vera specie,

zooming past our bewildered eyes like a child's
toy propeller plane darting up into the sky
then swooshing down – with the single purpose
of savoring the sweet ambrosia of orange trumpet
creepers or violet butterfly bushes

one moment here for us to enjoy, the next –
   while I run for my camera – magically invisible –
   a beauty that can sleep in the palm of my hand.

The Bamboo

The bamboo is always a beauty to behold
as it gracefully yields to the wind's multiple games,
showing innate resilience of temperament.

I wonder if it sighs along with the wind's wail,
strong as a spear, yet bending –
ceding like an archer's supple bow.

I can see its smooth surface gripped tightly
in the hands of an ancient Chinese warrior,
its emerald leaves like arrow heads ready to strike.

Yet they only quiver when the mischievous wind
shakes them, turning their elegant upright
spines into courteous humble bows.

Oh that our spines could mimic this playful sway
yielding, adapting, bowing,
and then, proudly straightening back up.

Garden Spider

Way above our heads, unreachable,
Our garden spider sleeps content –

Suspended on his barely visible silk hammock
Proud of weaving his own designer web

Week after week, getting fatter
with every snare

Enamored just to gaze out
at the turquoise dome above

Oblivious to all earth's infighting.

My Trees and I

Giant platanus trees in my Shemiran garden
You are of both worlds

Bound to the good earth,
Anchored to God's Nature,

You rise to the heavens,
Arms outstretched in adoration and praise

To God's magnificent creation,
You have been a witness

To the joys and sorrows of my life,
Always there, always in the present,

Full of beauty and life,
For thirty plus years

You have been my faithful friends
In all of life's ups and downs,

I have walked alongside your comforting arms,
Felt your powerful empathy,

Your soothing majestic presence,
Always an example to me

To stay the course and be strong,
To open my arms

Up to heaven like you –
And cry out: "How magnificent is Thy creation!"

The Zen Duck

It's near lunch time, and I'm walking in Renaissance
Park
a manicured park with large ponds, odd-shaped stones

and picturesque cascading waterfalls;
A mallard duck is standing motionless like a statue

on one of his short sturdy legs, probably napping,
his yellow beak lost in the pillow of his soft feathers

his glossy turquoise head glowing in the sunlight
his body oblivious to the noisy surroundings;

He's standing on a large stone around which strong
water currents are passing through his webbed foot,

He is in this calm repose just above a waterfall
as big for him as Niagara Falls, yet he's in peace;

I sit on a near-by bench, curious – watching,
none of the other ducks copy or join him there,

Is he a leader or a misfit loner who meditates?
I come back two hours later and he's still there

on the same one-legged immobile stance
I wonder if the drake will tire of this position

or did he shift his webbed feet while I was away?
The other ducks are all doing what ducks usually do:

swimming, head dipping, dabbling, sleeping, feeding,
enjoying a bath, or playing tag with one another,

I wonder whether this 'meditative' duck
is a 'Zen' duck or has reached "duck enlightenment?"

Annual Jousting

They brandish their lances –
branches with buds on one side,
the other with icicles,

The magnolias are peeping out
of their pearly spring hoods
oblivious to winter's secret snare,

No time to run for cover –
the treacherous frost gallops in
turning them into half frozen brown rolls,

The icy dew on the grass twinkles
like diamonds skillfully sown
on Mother Earth's emerald tapestry,

Even the early red buds
who dared show their purple lips
want to snuggle back

into their micro-pink cribs
dreaming to be opened
by the sun's passionate kisses,

this annual jousting of winter and spring
shall pass away with a short
or extended fighting farewell,

and spring will warm winter's cold lips
saying: "I shall surely see you next year –
I'll try to be punctual."

Like Magic but Real

Nature always seems to have its act together
never missing a single performance or cue
as we are apt to do;

We watch the unfolding, unrehearsed acts
one after another without intermission –
never boring, year after year;

Spring takes our breath away
it's fragrant breeze brings back
our frozen hopes oven-warm;

Summer's vibrant hues
are coveted candy or grandma's
colorful crocheted quilt;

The flaming fall leaves like bedlam dance
on glowing coal spells of a witch's cauldron
setting fire to hearts already bursting;

Winter's shimmering branches like spears
making us covet the sparkling diamonds –
to adorn just one long necklace,

like magic – but real.

Nature's Ways

If we quietly learn from Nature
we hurry no more

Dawn and dusk take their time
so do the seasons

Nature always deliberates at leisure
acting as if she had all eternity

Every detail is measured with care
every leaf, every flower takes its own time

Nothing is rushed or delayed
it is our hands that confuse the seasons

There is an infinite organizing
yet incomprehensible power

Nature's fingers match all with perfection –
constant motion and rest taking their time

A continual cycle of orderly change
Nature needs not boast

Her breathtaking beauty is there for all to see
her presence – here for us to feel

Nature never ceases to amaze or awe us
the stunning variety, the shifting colors

And what are we doing to her sacred beauty?
while Nature nurtures us, we betray her

We are inseparable as mother and child
yet even as we are held in her bosom

We toy with and forsake her
not knowing that we have

no other mother to turn to.

One with All

Fly and float with the snowflakes
Swing and sway with the autumn leaves

Feel their innocent freedom
Sense their inevitable fate of falling

Lie in the tiny bursting spring buds
And feel their effortless births

Be one with the wind that blows them
And feign their carefree non-attachment –

That sense of belonging anywhere –
Wherever Nature takes them

Masquerade as a golden daffodil or purple iris
Then as a pink peony, a red rose or geranium

Climb into the yellow tulip or red poppy
Clothe yourself with every beautiful flower

Savor each role – revel in the dream –
Embrace Nature's flowing show

Be many different "me's" every spring!

A Love Affair with the Moon

I, too, have a love affair with the moon
like Li Po who in innocent drunkenness

embraced the moon's reflection while boating
on a lake and drowning in the process –

leaving his orphan poetry to target hearts;
man has stepped on the glowing face,

walked on its rocky profile
uninvited yet intent on conquering,

my love affair seems one-sided –
I must hunt for another to hug.

Somersaulting Colors

It's autumn again and they are free to fly and float –
no longer restrained to their safe branch homes

they glide, twirl and somersault
like Olympic gymnasts of windy nations

some hold hands in flight like bird wings touching
or rubbing noses together in glee

all of them do it no matter what their color
free to fly as planes do in air shows

having abandoned their spring-summer habitat
they are partying, dancing together in their colorful
skins

it's a kissing time too – time to say farewell
as they tumble head over heels

till they huddle together at mother nature's earthen table
a "last supper," before their final farewells freeze over.

The Tree

The tree mourns not losing its leaves
it knows they'll be back,

It greets every season with open arms, proud –
always content – whether naked or clothed,

Its powerful roots safely sunk deep into the earth
and it's many arms uplifted, pointing in prayer

It lives in infinite faith – fearless and fulfilled.

The Sun and Shadows

The eerie beauty of the sun and shadows
Playing magic hide and seek

Like two enamored lovers
Flirting with each other

Enacting their harmonizing tai chi together
They take turns dominating

Even though the sun is master
One seems to flow into the other

Yet they do not struggle or compete
They just enjoy their tango of light and gray

Two in one.

Reminiscing on Spring

Spring buds appear like little knots
tied by mother nature's creative fingers
slowly she unties them

One
by
One

creating the ballet
of the blossoms, releasing
their sweet fragrance

Trees begin to show off their
fan-like emerald fingers, gracing us
with their comforting shade

Flowers rise up in rebellious colors
awakened from their deep sleep
by the sun's fiery kiss

What magic the Divine Magician
conjures up every spring –
just for us!

A Painting Contest

The contestant knows his icy arsenal is limited
A display of shades of grey everywhere
Sheets of glistening ice mirrors,

White paint drips from winter's master brush
Turning trees into Christmassy silver whites
Covering bare branches like cake icing or cream

Piles of it everywhere –
Like shiny white satin
Or fluffy cotton candy

It's fairyland all over again
Winter tries and tries, shivering all over
Everything is still snow white

Like the Pope's immaculate robe
He tries star designs on clouded windowpanes
The white paint covers equally all that is,

The contestant twirls white flakes into freezing rain
It only transforms to transparent whitish grey,
Cold winter's tears freeze on his icy cheeks

Only spring's warm and gentle hands of color
Will save winter from the clutches of its cold claws;
And then it's spring's turn to show off her art in color

First the rain must wash and melt the white away
Spring knows green is going to rule and reign,
So she digs through her arsenal of green shades:

Light green, moss green and forest green,
Shiny emerald, jade green for grasses and leaves
Spring remembers she mustn't run out of greens,

Then the blossoms must be softly colored
The most fun being creating the dancing flowers
Is this another paragon of paradise again?

Does shy spring know she has won the contest again?

Spring is Back Again

Spring is back again with its paint brush ready –
once again visualizing its painting spree

in its memory files of color-design creation:
what to paint when and what shades to use,

All conceivable colors lie waiting in its painting kit
with the impatient greens most important,

Smell the fragrance of earth and grass after rain,
behold the sun's awakening the sleepy flora,

Witness the wind's waltz with tibouchinas,
playing seesaw with emerald-studded branches,

Baby green leaves whispering: "We are back!"
Bees and blossoms in love again, tenderly kissing,

Butterflies and flowers beginning their annual romance
and spring's tender heart singing of resurrections,

Spring – the creator and witness of beauty
teaching lessons in miracles.

The Treacherous Freezing Rain

The treacherous freezing Iowa rain,
Pours from the grey pale sky,
Turning stunned children
Into skidding spins and pirouettes,

Unsuspecting tires into whirls and swirls,
Dictating like a pitiless brutal tyrant,
Ruling heaven and earth today,
Its glacial breath paralyzing trees,

Twisting branches into knifelike claws,
Like teeth on a witch's icy comb,
Or a carved pumpkin mouth,
With jagged sneering icicle teeth

Hurling branches to their destruction:
Is it a preview of an ice age?
But no, we have global warming,
So it's just a showing off of winter's prowess?

Stalactite icicles, gemlike pendants
Like diamonds on silver branch chains
Fooling us into believing its fairyland
Or one of the weather god's nasty tricks

Parading its spell of glittering pageantry?
No, there's no silver-lining this winter –
It's all fake, "fool's silver" masquerading….
Just jolting defenseless travelers

Before yielding with frigid vengeance
To spring's gentle grace.

The Weeping Willow Tree

The weeping willow tree in my Fairfield front yard
Always makes me smile – just looking at it

It reminds me of delicate Persian miniature paintings:
Lovers holding a cup and jug of wine under the tree

Or standing close together with one playing the sitar
Under this tree also called the *majnoon* tree

Every time I look at it, some branches seem to be
Waving at me with their whip-like swinging arms

There is always some activity going on –
The wind playing swing with its thin drooping
branches

My two squirrels chasing each other up and down
And me – laughing and taking pictures as though
They were my own two mischievous children

I think something is eating at the heart of my
willow tree
Half of it is drying up, although part of it seems
lively and well

I doubt whether my tree and squirrels missed me
As much as I missed them while I was gone

Now only one squirrel remains and he seems lonely
like me.

The Squirrel

Squirrels – they seem
  To live in the moment
    Unlike most of us,

Preoccupied with the
  Search for food
    And enjoying it or

Just having fun
  Whether in scampering,
    Climbing trees or

Chasing another squirrel,
  Their wiry strong paws
    Always empowering them

For climbing or digging sprees,
  Eating, or just shelling nuts
    And their elegant fluffy tail –

Like a grey- brownish
   Furry fanlike umbrella
      Protecting them from rain,

Quick and cautious –
   They make us stop and chuckle
      Glaring at us with curious suspicion,

Always occupied, whether nibbling,
   Hunting or having fun running –
      Planning for the future, scouting

In trees or combing, probing the earth,
   Digging, hiding precious nuts
      For future winter feasts.

The Web

A work of art –
the spider's silvery web
Every silky thread
crafted to capture
and enslave –
to kill.

Falling

spring blossoms open then fall
summer flowers shine then dry and fall

autumn leaves turn color then fly and fall
winter's bare tree branches await falling snow

days and years seem to fall faster
are we all in fast fall?

The Paradox

Does the hummingbird have two faces?
The one we usually witness,
the sweet side,
the magical picture –
its sucking the flower's nectar?
We are happy –
it's getting its vital nourishment.

Then there's the other side,
the violent side.
In mating, the male
attacks its rival
for the attention of its favored mate
with the same sharp weapon it uses to feed,
except here it stabs,
bloodying its opponent
as in a duel

in this strange game of courtship.

Droplet

Droplet on bamboo
Swaying in rhythm with wind
A moment – it leaps.

The Bee's Flirtation

The bee's flirtations
        flower's constant surrender
two dance a romance.

Windows

In this last section, I would like to share with you some of the dominant events that stand out in my mind's eye: colorful snapshots of my life. I recall stirring memories of my Mom and Dad. The happy memory of my first ballet class, and also, the emotional story, eighteen years later, when I found out my dance teacher was gone forever. I open the windows to the moving story of Ebony, my black piano, the impact my studies on China and living in Hong Kong has had on my life, and finally, life experiences divided between colorful Carlsbad, California and peaceful Fairfield, Iowa.

My Angel "Belle"

In stillness I sat meditating
    yearning to know my guardian angel

I called out to her –
    I called with heart and soul

my heart went still –
    I felt her presence

I asked her name
    and in the blissful stillness

came the amazing answer
    "Belle" – my name is "Belle!"

Bell as in "jingle bell"
    or "belle" as in French for "beauty?"

I know not which –
    the answer never came

yet deep within me
   there seems to be

an inner vision to the unseen –
   I can sometimes hear her

in silence,
   with my heart and soul.

My Beloved Mom

If I return again to this earth,
I want to be back with my Mom while she's cooking

my favorite saffron-colored rice with chicken, barberry,
and raisins. And I'll sit at the table and listen

to her counseling me with that irrepressible chuckle
of hers:
"Be kind and loving. Brave and strong like a lioness
of a woman,"

she'll tell me. Then, quoting Rumi: "With love,
thorns turn into roses!" and I'll be 18 again, she will
be happy

and cancer free. Healthy, beautiful, as she always was,
with that ever present loving smile on her beautiful face.

The Weeping Stream

My eyes have turned into a trickling stream
the heart cries along, overflowing –
both braid in sorrow on their way to the soul:

that is how a daughter feels
when the final separations come

you are never ready for the farewell –
you have lived as though they would live forever

all the feathers have been plucked from your wings
or maybe you no longer have any wings

in time you discover you can still sing with the birds,
the wind, the rain, and hum the melodies they loved

you learn to laugh at life's many pratfalls
and comedies even as the stream

in your eyes continues to trickle
to wash the burrowed sorrow inside

and even if you can no longer fly, you go on living –
in the wetness and sometimes the cold

living the way they wanted:
loving, hoping, dreaming, sometimes singing,
and, yes, even dancing now and then.

Echoes of My Father's Words

I look at the smiling picture of my father
  smoking his favorite corncob pipe

And I still remember him saying:
  "I want you to smile – always,

I want you to be strong – always."
  These echoes of my father's voice

Resonate in my ears every day:
  "*Festina Lente!*" says my father

With his understanding grin:
  "Yes, make haste, slowly!"

My fingers hurry to finish writing
  The maxim slides into my work

And keeps me from being rash
  I try to read all that I have left to read

I slow down and try to comprehend
    I hasten to muddle through my cooking

Then decide to slow down for quality
    I step on the gas in a mad rush

And again I hear his voice:
    "*Festina Lente*, daughter!"

These precious treasures I keep
    hidden in my heart to sustain me

When I seem to lose faith or hope –
    they leap into my consciousness

So I continue to smile –
    with strength to go on....

And I try to make haste, but – slowly.

My First Ballet Class

No ballet shoes my size
  My feet are too small at 3

The Russian shoemaker smiles:
  "I'll make you some soon," he says

I go barefoot into my first class
  Everybody else has ballet slippers

I timidly stand in the corner and wait
  My Polish-Russian ballet teacher smiles at me

She comes and picks me up lovingly
  Takes me to her bedroom and offers me

A piece of chocolate shaped like a fish
  Wrapped in shiny green paper

Mme Cornelli carries me back to the classroom
  Placing me in the very front row

I copy my beautiful teacher's movements
    Oblivious to my chubby bare feet

I am going to learn to dance –
    Nothing else matters.

Ebony

She was black, delicately beautiful, and born
in Germany in the late 19th century.
Place of residence was recorded as St. Petersburg
where she was dispatched in her infancy
to the royal courts of the Russian Czar.
For twenty years, the exquisite tones of Ebony's
ivory keyboard enchanted court audiences.

Then the brutal Bolshevik Revolution swept Russia
away
where devoted friends helped her escape
the chaos and ruthlessness, protecting and hiding her
during the revolution and in both devastating
world wars until a Russian-Polish ballerina fell in love
with her, taking her on the long hazardous journey
to Persia where she lived in the ballerina's dance studio.

We heard her harpsichordian tones thrice a week
for five years while we danced. But she grew older,
her wooden hammers weakening. My ballet teacher
was considering selling her off: "Would you buy her
for me?" I begged my hesitant parents.
Mother sold her diamond wedding ring to buy Ebony.
For over twenty years, I took good care of my piano,
loving, polishing, and playing her.

Then I had to leave Ebony for four years
when I made Hong Kong my home.
She was irreplaceable, but I needed to buy
another piano there. So when another revolution came
to the doors of my Ebony in 1979, I returned home
with my newer brown Yamaha.
I had to make a choice between the old and the new,
as there was no room in the house for two pianos.

So Ebony had to go, for she had aged beyond repair.
How could I save and protect my beautiful Ebony?
I owed it to her. In the dark of the night, a young
musician came with five friends, and the six had hell
carrying her out. I don't think Ebony wanted to leave.
She was going to play her tunes in a secluded
basement where an underground band composed
taboo Persian rock music.

String of Puns*

His stupid string of puns
From my one and only son
Not knowing he was annoying
He just kept on rowing
Until he saw my gun !

* This a limerick I wrote in jest
To put the rhythm to the test
to poke fun at my Son
when he was not at his best!

A Sweet Tongue

"A sweet tongue
brings love and endearment,

enticing even a snake
out of its hole,"

my Mom used to say,
"And a bitter tongue

makes you look ugly,
unloved and alone;

so take your pick,
my dear daughter!"

Immortality

Just back home from college in
the summer of 1963, I climbed
the familiar steep stone stairs carrying
a bouquet of bright red gladiolas

to her second floor studio, something
I had done for sixteen years
there was no answer when I knocked
at her door and the old Armenian shoemaker

next door blurted out in tears that she
had died up there in a fire three days ago.
I wept in open unashamed despair knowing
I would never see Madame Cornelli again

that treasure of my childhood memories, my
graceful ballet teacher with loving blue eyes
I had adored my entire life, a Polish-Russian
immigrant fleeing the USSR with her Italian

husband now dead, the handsome Renato,
her only son, an addict and in prison
I remember how she loved him and
how he came to take money from her

after which she would get migraines, tying
a white or blue chiffon scarf on her forehead
and how we knew we had to be very good
in class that day for her sake –

teaching us every dance move with passion
and precision, whether plies or pirouettes
she mirrored the miracle merging of
mind-body-spirit through dance and music

showing us what loving what you do meant,
and that beauty in life could be created
her outer shell may have turned to ashes,
yet she lives in every student she trained

touched by her wand of love,
she succeeded in creating
bliss and beauty in the picture
book of her students' memories.

When I dance alone,
I feel she is watching.
Is this immortality?

My China Life

When I come back this time,
I want it to be in China,
I'll wish to return as a painter
of haunting landscapes and a poet,

I shall ride my vermilion red pet dragon
over Jiuzhaigou, Guilin, and Hangzhou,
hovering over Fujian's Daoist
temples on Mount Wuyi and Hua Shan,

We will each have, my dragon
and I, a large green jade
medallion around our necks
for protection, just in case,

We shall build our home
near Huangguoshu waterfall
and explore the sacred
Mt. Emei, my dragon and I,

While he sits at the entrance
warming my house with his fiery breath,
I will stand at my painting desk
looking out, dreaming,

Imagining my poems, in beautiful,
bonelike black characters
dancing across the white
human size scrolls,

I shall wash my pet and tickle
him under the chin
maybe I will compose
poems like Li Po

Before he drowned while trying
to embrace the moon's reflection
and then I'll ride my faithful
dragon into the sunset

as Lao Tze did after
writing the *Dao De Jing*.

The Lady in a Garden

The most cherished treasure from Hong Kong
A picturesque 1850s antique painting on glass

Painted with love by an unknown Chinese artist
Memories of the Charlotte Hoerstmann exhibition

Where I fell in love with "The Lady in the Garden"
And paid for it dearly for the next four years

If the Virgin Mary could be Chinese she would
Look like this lady in a Chinese garden or

Maybe she is a beautiful Chinese empress –
I see an aura of grace all around her

Trees, shrubs, and flowers seem to bow to her
She stands chaste and tall, one hand caressing her
hairdo

Her china face looks immaculate, her expression pure
She is pale and tranquil, her long gown in delicate
pink

With flower designs on the fringes of her robe
A red tied bandeau cascading to the ground

Delicate long flowing reddish pink sleeves
With an intricate border of flower brocade

She smiles not, yet she is not sad, an air of poise
Of inward composure, equanimity encompasses her

Exuding a gracious portrait of beauty, refinement,
A quality of serene secrecy surrounds her

I wish my lady in the garden could tell me her story.

Sounds of Hong Kong

Street vendors cry out in wavy Cantonese as
throngs of tourist-shoppers slowly move along

Talking, arguing, bargaining in 'Chinglish' accents with
exclamations of '*ay-yaaaa*' and '*mo-waaaa*' everywhere

Inside buildings, claustrophobic elevators are
saturated
with the deafening volume of high or low- pitched
tones

Hour after hour, the Star Ferries' docking noises signal
back and forth trips between Hong Kong and
Kowloon

Fog-piercing shrill whistles of ship horns
accompany
sound of waves splashing against the crowded harbor

The plastic clicking and clacking of Mahjong games,
screeching trams with their magnified Tinker Bells

Children screaming and happily swimming in the
murky waters of Hong Kong, the "Fragrant Harbor"

Vendors' loudspeaker voices each compete for attention
enticing tourists to buy exotic China goods and
antiques

Restaurants full of people drinking tea, ordering
specialties
like shark fin or snake soup, and then burping away

Wails of tofu vendors with giant pots on bicycles or
shouting matches of those selling octopus meat

In the fish market, a cacophony of shrill voices
announce sales of every kind of seafood imaginable

strong smells and sounds zigzag for miles bringing
back vivid memories of this city of over 6 million –

One gigantic crowded shopping mall –
I relive the Hong Kong experience

every time I take out the packet
of sounds and smells frozen in time.

The Cave

The night was a nightmare with
   thoughts pounding in my drowsy crown,
    banging like scared bats
    against a cave's walls,

a cave whose mouth seemed sealed,
   the bats went dizzy in my head
    each with its own shrill shriek,
     every one vying for my attention,

I wished they would go into deep sleep
   like Rip Van Winkle, except upside down,
    leaving me in peace.

Sleep finally bore silence but
   in the early hours of the morning
    as I strained to wake the brain,

each bat in my head was still there,
   clinging to its side of the brain:
      "Could I begin one tranquil day?"

But once awake, the constant
   bat battle begins again, each thought
      weaving its own flight pattern,

its version of action-reaction,
   and the mind thinking itself powerless,
      surrendering to every thought,

thinking the cave entrance is sealed.

A Walking Stage Show

From my happy sunlit kitchen in Fairfield
I watch an endless stream of pedestrians trudging by

Auditioning for their roles in a walking stage show
Some walk with a determined rhythmic stride

As if supreme lord or headed for the top of the stack
A woman hobbles along like an old Chinese with
bound feet

Another treads along as though on treacherous ice
Others seem sluggish as in a slow motion dream

Some march with soldier-like precision, chin up
A lady limps away as if pinched by fate

And the routine boredom's of the day
Sorrows seem to sit on some stooped shoulders

As they plod under the weight of injustices
Some stroll with indifference, whistling, hands in
pockets

Others advance in confidence in a measured pace
Like the world owes them a gold mine or two

Still some seem to promenade with good cheer,
Smiling lovingly at you, at her, at him, at me

I wonder how each would see me
As I walk down the path of life.

"O wad some Power the giftie gie us
To see ourselves as ithers see us."*

*From *To a Louse,* by Robert Burns

The Return

In Fairfield, when I step outside my house –
I feel it is a mere extension of my home,

I've returned again to where I yearned to return,
It feels like I am walking a path of contentment,

I am happy here, in my home, in my town,
I savor the sweet nourishment of freedom,

The warm vibration of quiet secure familiarity
In this blessed Iowa bubble called Fairfield

Life is simple and uncomplicated here,
Meditation, kindness, and tranquility reign

I pilot my life the way I want – this way, that way
I listen to what the inner voice fancies –

In tune with my heart's irresistible impulses
My thoughts and feelings knit in peaceful harmony

This is my kind of town –
There must be some deep reasons why

Oprah called it "the most unusual town in America."

The Carlsbad Dancing Movers

I am watching from my upstairs bedroom window,
two of them are here: one with thick grey hair
and a Stalin-like mustache, the other, young, brawny,

moving their strong arms like dancing puppets
up and down, sideways and diagonally,
bones, muscles working as iron pulleys,

emptying well-packed brown boxes along with their
sweat
on the hot pavement, mingled with a crimson drop
of a cut,
they seem to be doing their own spirited dance

in careful calculated moves or rhythmic pantomime,
fingers reaching for nails, nuts and bolts to use
as old ladies would, digging into their sewing kits,

hands sometimes lifting like weight lifters in contests,
feet bending, straightening, stretching in slow motion
so synchronized and in harmony, like *tai chi*
students –

there is no harshness here, only gentle strength,
their faces seem satisfied, as though they are
enjoying it all – a kind of volunteering to serve

to lighten the burden of those who have just moved
in.

Face to Face

Face to face with death –
she left us forlorn

I cried and wept
cursed fate and pined

nothing happened –
only my wings broke

hope, faith left too
I smiled and tried

like she taught me –
I wrote a book

dedicated to her
I smiled and laughed

I wrote poems again
Hope, faith returned

My wings got strong
Mom was there smiling.

Carlsbad Fires

The world around
of breaking rules
is trial by fire
no time for defense

Dragon-mouth flames rising
then sinking in their bed of ire
by yellow-armored valiant knights
in the silence of the cliff's edge

The god of fire bullies you –
the driving force in dead heat
burning hearts and hopes.

Born to darkness or light
step on the fire cracking and
be the final witness.

The faithful fugitive full moon is
your second guardian angel.
Folly of the fathers blazes on

bringing drunken fear to a head –
the first unintended offense
revealed brightly in the veil of the night.

The chasing sun follows the never
ending cross of the seasons, now dry
and a fire's comeback bullies you
to guard the treasure of Self.

The earth's heir brings glad tidings
to divide the seeds of creation
a fall from grace can
turn the whisper red hot.

The angel says
time enough for love and fire
to get out of control.

Your vision can be cloud white
or charred black.

Time Slips through My Fingers

Time slips through my fingers
  Like live fish trying to get away
    An albatross around my neck

The seasons don't wait for me
  There is no intermission here
    They come and perform as they please

The years zoom by in a flicker of time
  And before you know it your hair is grey
    If you don't bother to color it

Your joints, swollen, creaky,
  Reminding you of your grandmother's
    Your hands unsteady, a little shaky

Like Dad's mild Parkinson's
  And you are not ready to go yet
    You have not written all you wanted –

On the tablet of your destiny.

Treasure of Memories

Persepolis and the poetry of Rumi and Hafez – Persia
pavilions, palaces, bicycles – China
rolling fields of corn and soy beans – Iowa
iridescent hummingbirds – California

intricate beauty of Persian carpets and miniatures
dancing calligraphy and brush paintings of China
farm houses and scampering squirrels of Iowa
endless flower festivals of California

ancient cultures gifted with breath-taking natural
beauty
younger ones have the beauty of Nature minus what?

A Hafez Poem

"If the beloved can win my love and grant me kindness
so my arms can circle round her neck

I'd give away all of Samarkand and Bokhara
for the beauty spot on her face

My heart would leap for joy
just for a passing glance of her eyes

And I'd bow down, sweeping with my eyebrows
the sacred ground she stands on

Give me cup-bearer, the eternal wine
that you can't even find in heaven

Just keep your heart away from pensive thoughts
for the lover's destructive charms can conquer

Your heart and rob the soul's peace as invading
conquerors like the Tartars did...."*

How much are we willing to give
for the love of the beloved?
Our possessions, our all in life
or only the intangibles – that really cost us nothing?

Hafez says he's willing to give away cities
not his to give away
just for a beauty spot on the beloved's countenance
But can we dispose of things not ours?

Isn't it easy to do that?
And harder to give with heart and soul
what's truly ours?

* The first part of this poem is my translation of the
third ode (ghazal) of Hafez, the second, are some of my
comments on it.

Dream Daughter

She rises with a twinkle in her honey-colored eyes
reminding me of lurking mischief

Her tiny mouth somehow stretches into a pumpkin
grin
then closes like a shy pink spring bud

Her golden hair blows in the wind like fall's yellow
leaves
she carries herself with the graceful posture of a dancer

Lily looks as though she has just walked out of
Leonardo da Vinci's "A Child's Luxuriant Head of
Hair,"

She runs to you in blissful adoration
humming her favorite tunes as if on stage

Takes her seat at a white harpsichord, playing like
Mozart
she is my dream daughter in the next life

In this one, a son has blessed me.

For Grandsons

Grab someone's attention –
   your own is usually best

An extraordinary opportunity
   can come kicking in anytime – grab it

If you ever happen to fail
   there's always a next time—

If you hang in there like a pro –
   always time for new beginnings

Dig in and decide
   to stay the course

You can crack any nut
   despite the tough climb

Keeping cool and focusing
   on the chessboard is half the battle

Surrender does not exist
  in your dictionary

And sorrow never finds
  a nest in your heart

Commit – and hurl wisely
  the preemptive strike

You can counter
  any invasion in your life

When you gradually see
  the light even through darkness

Gadflies may always be parading as heroes
  but your trusted self is the real hero

Never disenchanted, always passionate
  your motto is "enter," never "exit" –

Unless your work is done
  when the eleventh hour strikes.

The Dragon

The vermillion dragon painting hanging in my office
purchased during my Hong Kong sojourn
seems relentlessly after the pearl in the clouds
but whenever I look up from my desk
I see his fiery gaze as though following me
while his stare does not scare me in daylight
those piercing eyes do unnerve me in the evenings
his four-fingered claws always seem poised
in his quest of snatching the pearl of wisdom.
This dragon takes me to another dimension –
away from life's mundane routines to that
of magical dreams and mythical tales,
of dragon slayings or friendships.
What I see and feel day in and day out
is the dragon's constant message to me:
"Search for the prized pearl of knowledge."

Can I do that for me?

Lights

Glowing fireflies at night
Flashes of lightning
The glitter of Christmas lights
A quivering shimmer of a candle

For me, the best light
apart from the sun,
the sparkle
in my grandson's eyes.

www.ingramcontent.com/pod-product-compliance
Lightning Source LLC
Chambersburg PA
CBHW022011090426
42741CB00007B/980